THE WAY OF THE SOUL®
The Path To Self Empowerment

Author Ross Bonacci ©
Artist Heidi Meuwissen©
www.thewayofthesoul.com

POST CARDS FROM THE VOID

Author Ross Bonacci ©

Artist Heidi Meuwissen©

POST CARDS FROM THE VOID

Balboa Press books may be ordered through booksellers or by contacting:

Balboa Press
A Division of Hay House
1663 Liberty Drive
Bloomington, IN 47403
www.balboapress.com
1-(877) 407-4847

Because of the dynamic nature of the Internet, any Web addresses or links contained in this book may have changed since publication and may no longer be valid. The views expressed in this work are solely those of the author and do not necessarily reflect the views of the publisher, and the publisher hereby disclaims any responsibility for them.

ISBN: 978-1-4525-3200-4 (sc)

Library of Congress Control Number: 2010919535

Any people depicted in stock imagery provided by Thinkstock are models, and such images are being used for illustrative purposes only. Certain stock imagery © Thinkstock.

Printed in the United States of America

Balboa Press rev. date: 1/26/2011

BALBOA.
PRESS
A DIVISION OF HAY HOUSE

Thank You

Thank you, for purchasing 'Post Cards from the Void'. It has been my absolute privilege and pleasure to present them to you.

These eleven 'Post Cards from the Void' take a deeper look at the human condition and how we fit into the larger scheme of things.

The Post Cards are part of 'The Way of the Soul',
Soul Card collection;

Acknowledgment

I would like to thank Maureen Smith and Amanda
Ahern for their loving guidance and inspiration.

A very special thank you goes to Heidi Meuwissen a truly gifted artist.
She is gifted beyond her years, and was guided to me by God. Her
artwork is timeless, as it captures the very meaning of life within its frame.

- Ross Bonacci founder/Author of The Way of the Soul

ROSS BONACCI / FOUNDER

THE WAY OF THE SOUL – about the author

Ross Bonacci has studied and explored numerous healing modalities and is a Master of Reiki, Zenith Omega, and Avatar. He has been on the path of self discovery since his late teens and his great appreciation for life has inspired an enquiry into the human potential. He confesses that his soul guided him on his travels.

His journey has taken him too many sacred places both within himself and also geographical locations around the world. He embraces a multi denominational view point on the Cosmos and all that is.

The Way of the Soul is the distillation of his many trainings and his experiential understanding of them. Ross now; humbly, yet proudly presents to you his offering of thanks to all those who have been part of his Evolution;

POST CARDS FROM THE VOID is his gift to you to honour and accelerate your journey home to yourself.

May this book guide you home with ease and grace; Ross resides in Sydney Australia. He is available for public lectures and teachings.

Heidi Meuwissen - About the Artist

Heidi Meuwissen has been painting since her early teens. Heidi's
love for art has grown stronger and stronger year by year.
She is passionate about color and bringing the healing
power of art to life with her unique style.
Born 11th September 1989 and raised in Sydney Australia
with a Dutch background, she attended Meriden
Anglican School and went on to further her studies in art
at National Art School in Darlinghurst Sydney [2008]

Heidi Achievements
Awards –
2010 - Liverpool art prize exhibition;
2009 - Selected Urban chalk pavement festival artist;
2007 - Senior lavender art and design prize.

Exhibition Groups
Liverpool Art Prize Exhibition, Chalk Pavement
Exhibition, HSC Art Exhibition;

Heidi's art comes from the heart. She has a very beautiful open loving
heart and is able to express her emotions though the journey of her art.
At the age of 21years she is truly an amazing gifted artist beyond
her years. Her artwork captures the meaning of life in its frame.

For more of Heidi's work visit her website at: www.heidimeuwissen.com
Post Cards from the Void introduces the following sacred
symbolic piece of art, intended to impart a sense of joy,
love and tranquillity into the heart of the reader.

The Post Cards were revealed to me as I
travelled the corridors of my inner self.

I discovered parts of myself that I had left behind. It is almost as if
they appeared to me, to assist in the recovery of my wholeness.
The Post Cards are here to help you forget what you have
learned and to remember what has been forgotten. They are
here to support you in the recovery of your wholeness.

Sometimes when we are so consumed with our daily lives, we
lose perspective of the bigger picture. It's as if we disconnect
from part of ourselves. What's happening in the world around
us? How does our universe fit in with other universes? By having
made that inner journey I hope I can offer some comfort to
those who follow and honour those who have been before.

Where the Post Cards came from

As I walked the corridors of my inner self, I discovered many things about myself, things that I'd forgotten, things that I had left behind. I guess the most interesting thing that happened was a very large ornate door appeared before me and it was labelled doorway to the Void. I went to open this door but it was locked. I tried to knock it down but it was rock solid. At that point I looked in my pocket and I found a key labelled doorway to the void.

I suddenly realised that I hold the keys to all things.

I unlocked the large ornate door. As I walked through the door a red sports car appeared before me and a man walked from the red sports car towards me. "Ahoy to you, you have arrived lets go for a ride!" My mind was racing with questions. What is your name? Who are you? What is this place? Could it be the doorway to the Void? What is that? What is the Void? Questions, questions, questions!?!

"My name is *I Am That I am*. Come on! Jump in! Let's go for a ride."
"That's an interesting name, you can call me Ross. Where are you taking me?" "To have coffee of course; **Cafe de Void** is the best cafe in town. It is located on boulevard of dreams come true. There are people there that would like to meet you. They are waiting for you."
"They knew I was coming?"
"Oh Yes. We have all been awaiting your arrival"
As we drove down Boulevard of dreams come true, I noticed that everything around me, the streets, the buildings, were all amazingly breathtaking. Houses made of gold, truckloads and truckloads of money, sports cars, and corporations with my name on them. Everything I had ever imagined, everything I had ever dreamed of was in this place. What a wondrous place to visit.
"What is this place?"
My guide who preferred to be called *I Am That I Am*, told me that this is the place where dreams are born.

Everything you have ever wished for rests within the Void.
The stillness, the vastness, of everything; I was experiencing there, was breathtaking.

We arrived at **Cafe de Void**. We walked inside the café. The cafe was abuzz with activities. Many interesting people and other beings were mingling and connecting as if there were no barriers to communication. Extra Terrestrials, Entities, Lost Souls, Dark Souls, all seemed to be having the time of their lives. *I Am That I Am* had a table prepared for us both to sit at. A roundtable with a red tablecloth with lounge like type chairs was laid out before us. Was this all pre ordained? I wondered. He ordered a piece of mud cake and cafe latte for both of us.

"There are many people here who wish to speak to you, many have messages, important things to say to you so listen well and take notes. You are to call this work **"Post Cards from the Void"**.

"Hmm. I like it." The first group of people who came to sit with me call themselves dark souls. I nearly fell off my chair. Imagine being able to speak freely with these creatures from the underworld and be completely safe. There were so many things I wanted to know. "Are you from hell or did the devil send you?" I enquired. To answer both of your questions - No! No! We are not. They told me who they were and where they come from they gave me a message.

DARK SOULS

There are dark souls amongst us

I would like you to be aware that there are dark souls who walk amongst us. These souls are not lost, for they know that they are dark souls. They do not fear the light and have no desire or wish to go to the light. What does one do if one of these souls crosses your path in spiritual form?

The same as you would, if such a person crosses your path in physical form. You do not interact with them or befriend them. If you see a ferocious animal in a cage you would not enter the cage, for you know if you did, you would get hurt. So be aware of the boundary you place around yourself and around others. Your boundaries keep you safe from these dark energies.

Intention: I have strong boundaries and I am safe

DARK SOULS

I have strong boundaries and I am safe

The second group of people who stepped up called themselves Lost Souls. They explain to me who they were and where they come from. I asked if they were related to the Dark Souls? "Yes, we are second cousins," they replied. They also had a message for me:

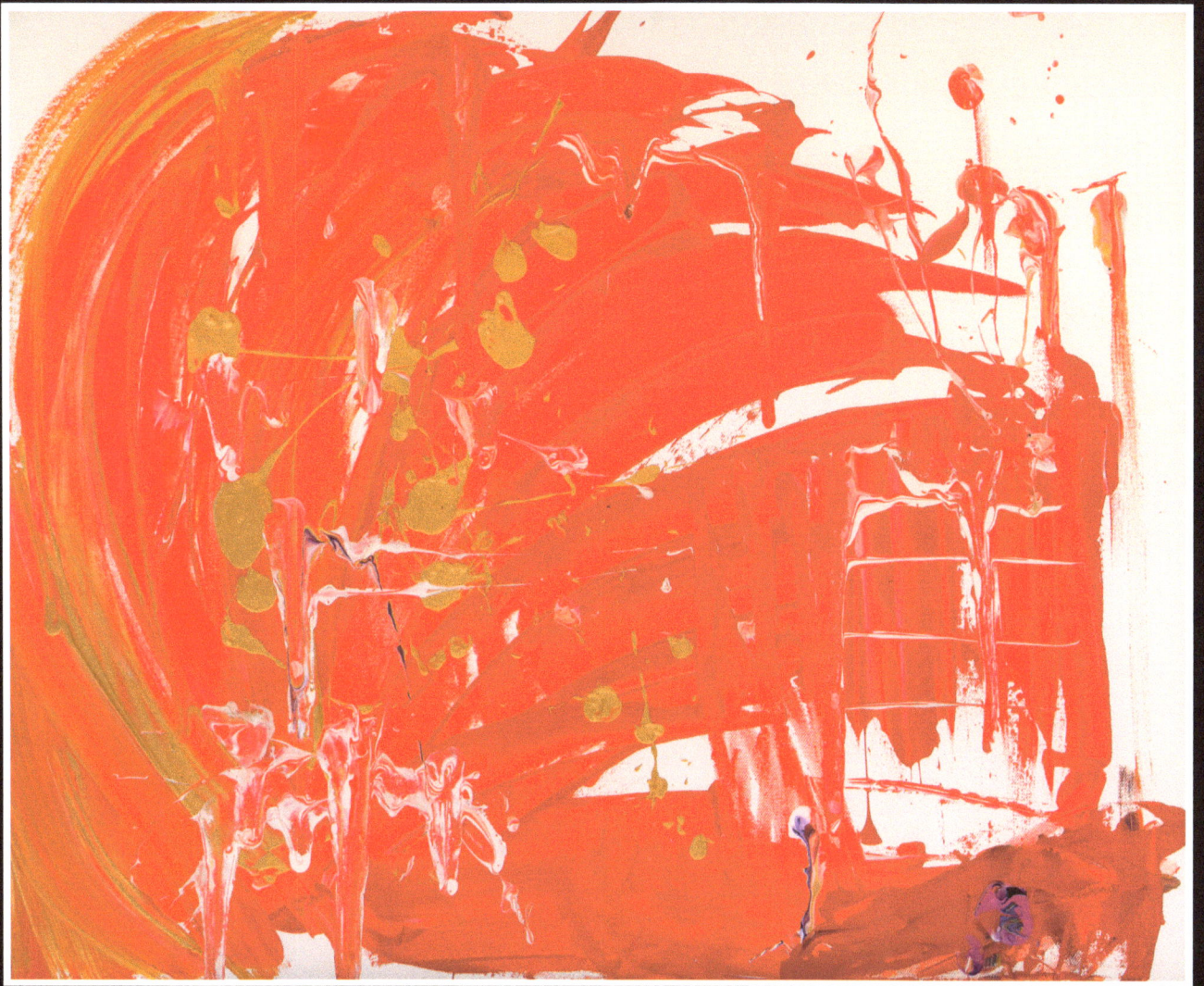

LOST SOULS

There are lost souls around you

Lost souls are people who were once in physical form but have now passed over. But now find themselves in a place which is unknown to them; a type of limbo. They are afraid of the light, so they sit in the shadows. They attached themselves to people in the living. They live in the fear of what is unknown to them; these souls can be quite mischievous. They affect the living in many ways. Have you ever considered whether the thoughts you are having are your thoughts or someone else's thoughts. The headache that came from nowhere, all signs that lost souls may be around you. Call upon the Archangel's to help these lost souls and you will provide a great service to all there is. The Archangels open the doors to the heavens. The Archangel's assist these lost souls in their crossing over.

Intention: May all beings live in the light

LOST SOULS

May all beings live in the light

The next group of people that stand before me called themselves Walk Ins. One soul walks into the body and one soul walks out of the body what an interesting concept, the Walk Ins said to me that there are literally thousands, hundreds of thousands of Walk Ins who sit in the spiritual realms waiting for their turn to come into the body. They explained to me the part they take in the evolution of consciousness.

WALK – IN

Your consciousness is about to radically change very quickly.

This is a life changing event and sometimes is quite difficult for the individual to go through. Your consciousness totally changes. You are not the same person you used to be even though the body looks the same. This is when two souls have made an agreement to switch places. When the first soul has gone as far as they can in their development in the physical form and they are ready to move on. One soul walks out, another soul walks in. Normally permission has been granted for this to take place before the body is born. This is also known as soul transference. Normally walk-ins are gifted light workers who come to this physical plane to do much spiritual work.

Intention: I am a being of light

WALK – IN

I am a being of light

The room suddenly filled with light. I could feel the grace of God. Mother Mary and Mother Teresa appeared before. "We have waited a long time to speak to you, young man." "Who me? Could this really be happening?" I thought. Yes, I could not only see them before me but feel the truth of what they were saying to me. I opened my self to receive their Messages as if I was a custodian of something truly sacred They spoke to me about helping those less fortunate, taking care of mother earth, caring for the sick and those who have lost their way.

HOLY MOTHER MARY

Mother Mary graces you with her presence.

I have waited a long time to speak to you. I have deep concern for your world; there is much fear and anger in your world. Be at peace with each other. Forgive each other, respect each other, love each other, live together in harmony. The time has come for you to let go of your fears and doubts that stand in the way of your power. Lead the way for others. This is the time for re-conciliation. Take time out from your busy lives. Take the time to pray. I ask the world leaders to be at peace with one another and work together to stop the fighting. Bring food to those that have no food. Provide shelter for the homeless. Take care of the sick, care for the dying. Help those who have lost their way. Take special care of mother Earth for she is your home. The divine light that you are shines the way for others. Mother Mary blesses you.

Intention: I embrace my role as a leader

I embrace my role as a leader

Mother Teresa then spoke to me, her voice gentle and soothing.

MOTHER TERESA

*Take the time to smell the roses
Take time out from your busy lives. Take the
time to look at the world around you.
When I look at your world; I see so many people are starving.
They have no food; no fresh water. They have no home or shelter.
So many people die each and every day of starvation. My heart
bleeds for their souls. For they are just like you, just trying to live life.
Smile, open your hearts help those less fortunate than yourself. How
can we help the millions of people in the world that are starving
and have no shelter or fresh water to drink? You start in your own
backyard. Make peace with your neighbour. Smile at each other.
Help each other. We are all family. We are all children of God*

Intention: I am a child of God and all people are my brothers and sisters

MOTHER TERESA

I am a child of God and all people are my brothers and sisters

Jesus and Mary Magdalena and their children were next.
"You two have kids," I exclaimed. "WOW!
Just wait until I tell the local minister back home"
Both Jesus and Mary Magdalena had beautiful
messages for me to bring back with me.

JESUS

You are eternal light beings.

I honour you. I have great respect for who you are. You are all walking in your light, even though you may not see it in this way. When you look at yourselves, you see the father, the mother, the child, the teacher, the postman, the policeman, the factory worker. These are all roles you have chosen to play on your human journey. When I look at you, what I see is internal light beings. You are beings who have come to this planet to have a human experience, a flesh and bone experience. I will assist you to connect with the divine, of which you are a part. I know you feel all alone. I know you all feel a great separation from all there is. I am here to help you reconnect with the divine; the greater wisdom and knowledge of all there is. This knowledge and wisdom can now travel through you. You are the educator. You have the capacity to teach others the way of the divine.

Intention: I trust my innate wisdom and divine nature

JESUS

I trust my innate wisdom and divine nature

MARY MAGDALENA

It is time embody the spirit of devotion

The union between the feminine and masculine aspects of self is occurring in your life. Many have said to you, that a new partner, a new relationship is coming into your life. But in truth what is actually occurring is the marriage of the female and male aspects of who you are. Mary Magdalene is assisting you with this process. She urged you to be patient with yourself and allow these two parts of self to blend with one another. Your inner union is reflected in your physical world. Your relationships with other people change. You no longer lose yourself within relationships. You become a free spirit. Your partner also aligns with you. If you are without a partner, he or she will appear to you and you will walk forward as two free spirits exploring life.

Intention: I am a free spirit.

MARY MAGDALENA

I am a free spirit.

The next group of people that came before me
were very difficult to describe or explain.
They were so different to us humans. Who are you?
You look so different to the human kind.
In your terms we're extraterrestrials, ETs, there are
many different species of extraterrestrials.
Open your mind to what there is out there. I was awestruck
by their appearance and their minds. I could sense they
knew my thoughts before I did. It was quite extraordinary,
yet I felt completely safe and it all felt natural.

EXTRATERRESTRIALS

Open your mind to other realms and possibilities

Alien life forms; do they exist? Alien abductions; do they really happen? Are we alone or are their other life forms on other planets, yes, yes, yes. Please do not be alarmed or afraid. You have asked for this information that is why it has been given to you. Expand your thinking beyond what you think you know. Be open to the possibility. What is there to be afraid of really?

Intention: The truth is greater than we think

EXTRATERRESTRIALS

The truth is greater than we think

Well are you ready for it?
The Wild Card was next. Yes, he called himself The Wild Card.
He told me "I represent everything and anything whatever you wish
to be. Both in physical and spiritual form; I hold the keys to the city.
Everything is possible. Whatever you wish to be, you can be."
Naturally I wanted to know where I can get a set of keys like that.

THE WILD CARD

This is your free pass; the keys to the city

You are the wild card. This represents everything and anything, whatever you wish it to be... Spiritually you hold the divine keys in your hands. You have access to any dimension, any reality that you wish to explore. Take a walk through the Akashic records. Your spiritual freedom is also reflected in your physical life. This also marks the completion of all things. Choose the direction that your heart desires to go in. In your physical life, this path opens up for you and there will be no obstacles. This is a free pass, both spiritually and physically. You have worked very hard to get to this point. You are rewarded on all levels. As it is in heaven so it is on earth.

Intention: All my efforts are richly rewarded

All my efforts are richly rewarded

Well by this stage I had had that much coffee
and cake that I was ready for a nap.

THE ENTITY THAT I AM

*It is time to recall your essential nature and
live it out with grace and gratitude.
Your essential nature is always present in your human
body and witnesses all you experience in life. Who is
watching the watcher? That constant vigilant awareness
of self is your entity inseparable from life itself.*

Intention: I am that I am.

THE ENTITY THAT I AM

I am that I am.

With that thought I woke up sitting in my lounge chair
at home it was 3 a.m. with the TV still blaring.
I had a very strong feeling come over me that
I had to write down my thoughts.
This was the birth of "Post Cards from the Void".

THE VOID

*Discharge all thoughts and doubts about your
ability to receive your dreams.*

*The void is the host to all that is. It is the container for infinity,
limitless possibilities, the womb of every creation past, present
and future. It is the omnipresent eternal NOW. It paradoxically
has no form and yet all form arises from it. It is the form of the
formless. The Void is the place where all dreams, thoughts, ideas
are born and grow and begin their journey home to you.*

Intention: I take ownership of my dreams

THE VOID

I take ownership of my dreams

I trust my innate wisdom and divine nature

Ross Bonacci ©

The truth is greater than we think

Ross Bonacci ©

THE END

www.ingramcontent.com/pod-product-compliance
Lightning Source LLC
Chambersburg PA
CBHW060806270326
41927CB00002B/71